A Purple Summer

A PURPLE SUMMER

Notes on the Lyrics of
Spring Awakening

Steven Sater

An Imprint of Hal Leonard Corporation

Published in 2012 by Applause Theatre & Cinema Books
An Imprint of Hal Leonard Corporation
7777 West Bluemound Road
Milwaukee, WI 53213

Trade Book Division Editorial Offices
33 Plymouth St., Montclair, NJ 07042

Based on the play *Frühlings Erwachen* (*Spring Awakening*) by Frank Wedekind.

All photos in the insert are from the 2010–2011 *Spring Awakening* national tour.

Printed in the United States of America

Book design by Mark Lerner

Library of Congress Cataloging-in-Publication Data is available upon request.

ISBN 978-1-55783-824-7

www.applausebooks.com

For my father

I still remember it so clearly, though it's almost as if it had happened to someone else: attending a performance of *Porgy and Bess* with Duncan, coming home, full of aspiration, and with the somber beauty of Gershwin's music still in my head, writing the first lyric of *Spring Awakening*: "Mama Who Bore Me." A lyric that still stands, just as I wrote it that night.

That was February 1999. Little could I have dreamed that I would sit today, in the spring of 2011, and begin writing notes on my own lyrics.

But . . . in working with the German translators toward our March 2009 premiere in Vienna, I wrote many e-mails, critiquing drafts and mapping routes and strategies for the translators to take. And in so doing, I (naturally enough) began explicating my lyrics.

And then, while reading those e-mails, my director for all these years, Michael Mayer, and our musical director, Kimberly Grigsby, began urging me to expand my notes and explain myself a bit.

After working with so many young actors through auditions, rehearsals, and performances, Michael and Kim felt strongly that such notes would be invaluable for maintaining the quality of future productions of our show, when those of us who created it would no longer be near.

Frankly, I found the suggestion startling and strange. I said to Michael, "What? Notes on my own lyrics? Like Eliot's 'Notes on "The Waste Land"'?" Michael's eyes widened and he grinned that inimitable grin: "Exactly."

"Mama Who Bore Me"
Wendla and Girls

Mama who bore me.
Mama who gave me
No way to handle things. Who made me so sad.

Mama, the weeping.
Mama, the angels.
No sleep in Heaven, or Bethlehem.

Some pray that, one day, Christ will come a'-callin'.
They light a candle, and hope that it glows.
And some just lie there, crying for him to come
*   and find them.*
But when he comes, they don't know how to go . . .

Mama who bore me.
Mama who gave me
No way to handle things. Who made me so bad.

Mama, the weeping.
Mama, the angels.
No sleep in Heaven, or Bethlehem.

My biggest issue with the German translation of this lyric proved insoluble for our premiere. Duncan so memorably set to music my opening word "Mama" that, all those years later, the words and music were as one. Everyone felt that those opening notes required the word "Mama." But, once that "Mama" was in place, there seemed no way, in German, for the opening line of our opening song to introduce the primary theme of our play: "Mama who bore me."

Further, our translators could find no way for Wendla's musings to hang, as they do in English, in a sort of suspended, wistful address. "Mama who" became "Mama, *du*" ("Mama, you"). And so, our Viennese production began with a young girl pointing the finger of blame at her mother: "Mama, *you* . . .don't feel the pain in my heart."

But this lyric was never meant as accusation. The text is simple and plaintive. The song is a sort of elegy the girl sings for herself. It's as if, in examining her maturing body in the mirror, she were also reviewing a portrait of her mother, the woman who bore her to the sad world within her.

Wendla is groping. She watches herself turn woman, and she has no language to make sense of it—only the Bible words of her child-life.

Some pray that, one day, Christ will come
    a'-callin'.
They light a candle, and hope that it glows.

The "candle" here alludes to the Parable of the Ten Virgins in Matthew 25. The maidens await the coming of the heavenly bridegroom, but some have neglected to take oil for their lamps. And so they must go refill them, and are no longer home when he finally comes to call.

But what if our bridegroom never shows? If the life we long for never finds us, what are we to do? What is our grown life to be, if we only wait for some illumination of the pain and it never arrives?

And what if, when our savior comes, we "don't know how to go"? Wendla yearns so badly to *understand*. She wants to feel, to know, what it means to be alive. And yet, her mother, Frau Bergman, is so flustered by the young girl's impropriety, in asking how babies are born, that the woman can only hide Wendla's head beneath her apron.

It's as if, within Wendla's heart, there were some silent cry: "Mama, you must help me, you must tell me . . .I hear only the weeping, the angels, and my heart won't be put to sleep by some would-be comforting thought of Heaven or Bethlehem."

The weeping, the angels, owe something to Shakespeare's Isabella (*Measure for Measure*), another innocent who pleads for understanding from a would-be righteous soul: "but man, proud man / Drest in a little brief authority . . . / Plays such fantastic tricks before high heaven / As makes the angels weep . . ."

Wendla stands before the mirror in a near-transparent dress. Even as she struggles to understand, she finds a guilty pleasure in her budding breasts, and already thinks of herself as somehow "bad."

"All That's Known"
Melchior

All that's known
In History, in Science,
Overthrown
At school, at home, by blind men.

You doubt them,
And soon they bark and hound you—
Till everything you say is just another bad about
   you.

All they say
Is, "Trust in What Is Written."
Wars are made,

And somehow that is wisdom.

Thought is suspect,
And money is their idol,
And nothing is okay unless it's scripted in their
    Bible.

But I know
There's so much more to find—
Just in looking through myself, and not at them.

Still, I know
To trust my own true mind,
And to say: "There's a way through this . . ."

On I go,
To wonder and to learning—
Name the stars and know their dark returning.

I'm calling,
To know the world's true yearning—
The hunger that a child feels for everything they're
    shown.

You watch me—
Just watch me—
I'm calling,
And one day all will know . . .

You watch me—
Just watch me—
I'm calling,
I'm calling,
And one day all will know . . .

This song was a long time coming, for we had to figure out first how best to launch Melchior's journey. I have written (in the preface to our published libretto) of how the lyric came into being backward. (If our show was to end with a boy learning the hard lessons of his heart, then it only made sense to introduce him as a guy with a naive pride in the power of his own mind.)

In Wedekind's great original play, we never see the boys (or girls) in school. We meet Melchior and Moritz leaving class, excusing themselves from their friends to walk in the woods and talk sex. For our musical, I constructed an entirely new scene, set in the classroom, the better to introduce our young rebel. The scene also allows us to see the repressive nineteenth-century German school system in operation: force-feeding young minds "a proper education," while quelling all the life in them.

It also allows us to see Moritz floundering in the classroom, rather than merely talking about it. When Professor Sonnenstich derides the "sleepyhead" for his faulty Latin recitation, Melchior stands up and defends Moritz's error as a "plausible conjecture." Thus, not only do we see Melchior's brilliant young mind in action, but also how far he will go, how much he will risk to try and help his friend. And the upshot? Melchior is himself chastised and brutally struck by Herr Sonnenstich.

As the boys resume their recitation of Virgil, we enter Melchior's mind with this song. In the front half of the lyric, Melchior decries the blindness of a parochial system (a "parentocracy") that willfully ignores the more enlightened discoveries of history and science for the sake of what is "scripted in their Bible."

He soon senses, though, that he resolves nothing by pointing his finger at others. Rather, he must look within himself—and trust in his own mind to transform the world around him.

> *But I know*
> *There's so much more to find—*
> *Just in looking through myself, and not at them.*
>
> *Still, I know*
> *To trust my own true mind,*
> *And to say: "There's a way through this . . ."*

If only it were that simple, and the world were ready to hear the cries of its young idealists and aright itself.

Over the course of his journey, Melchior will have his spirit broken by the System. He will come to feel totally fucked by the ways "this contemptible bourgeois society works." On his knees in a graveyard, he is ready to draw a razor across his throat, until he hears the voices of his lost friends and determines to live on, to carry forward their memory. The turning point of "All That's Known," and its counterpart at the graveyard toward the very end, "Those You've Known," is the stars.

On I go,
To wonder and to learning—
Name the stars and know their dark returning.

I'm calling,
To know the world's true yearning—
The hunger that a child feels for everything they're
*   shown.*

Here, Melchior resolves to leave behind the soul-infesting school system and learn from Plato's "Theaetetus": to pursue "the wonder" of the world with his own eyes—for, as Plato tells us, "Philosophy is born of wonder." So will Melchior "name the stars and know their dark returning." At story's end, it is these same stars that offer him a new start.

For me, these stars recall those that appear to the watchman at the beginning of Aeschylus' *Agamemnon.* As this lone guard crouches on the rooftop of the Palace of Atreus, waiting year after year for some signal that Troy has fallen and his lord is finally headed home, the stars bear him company and mark the passing of time.

In luminous nightly processions, they return to their appointed places in the dark heavens, bearing winter and summer to humankind.

So do the stars bear Melchior company, and tell of "spring returning," as he departs the graveyard. He determines to read to them the dreams of his lost friends, as he completes his journey from head to heart, from *all* that's known to *those* he's known.

"The Bitch of Living"

Moritz and Boys

God, I dreamed there was an angel, who could
hear me through the wall,
As I cried out—like, in Latin: "This is so not life at
all.
Help me out—out—of this nightmare." Then I
heard her silver call—
She said: "Just give it time, kid. I come to one and
all."

She said: "Give me that hand, please, and the itch
you can't control,

Let me teach you how to handle all the sadness in
     your soul.
Oh, we'll work that silver magic, then we'll aim it
     at the wall."
She said: "Love may make you blind, kid—but I
     wouldn't mind at all."

It's the bitch of living
With nothing but your hand.
Just the bitch of living
As someone you can't stand . . .

See, each night, it's, like, fantastic—tossing,
     turning, without rest,
'Cause my day's at the piano—with my teacher
     and her breasts;
And the music's, like, the one thing I can even get
     at all,
And those breasts! I mean, God, please, just let
     those apples fall . . .

It's the bitch of living
With nothing going on.

Just the bitch of living,
Asking: "What went wrong?"

Do they think we want this?
Oh—who knows?

See, there's showering in gym class . . .

Bobby Maler, he's the best—
Looks so nasty in those khakis . . .

God, my whole life's, like, some test.

Then there's Marianna Wheelan—as if she'd return
    my call.

It's like, just kiss some ass, man—then you can
    screw 'em all.

It's the bitch of living—
And living in your head.
It's the bitch of living,
And sensing God is dead.

It's the bitch of living
And trying to get ahead.
It's the bitch of living—

Just getting out of bed.

It's the bitch of living—
And getting what you get.
Just the bitch of living—

And knowing this is it.

God, is this it?
This can't be it.
Oh God, what a bitch!

This lyric feels so straightforward, I don't know that it calls for explanation. The earliest drafts of the German lyric, however, rendered it as a sort of ode to masturbation, which it really is not. "The Bitch of Living," which begins with Moritz's dreamed rendezvous with the Angel of Sex, is about something much broader—the nightmare of a nonlife.

Yes, the Angel of Sex assures Moritz that he is not alone in the dizzying world of "sticky dreams." She will teach him how to handle "all the sadness in his soul"—by aiming it squarely at the wall. Still, when day is done, he is left with no one, living as someone he can't stand: "Do they think we want this?" A life where the full, glorious view of our piano teacher's breasts leads only to further frustration? Further useless rebellious rage? "Oh—who knows . . ."

It is important to note that, in the bridge of the song, Ernst, Hanschen and Otto's remarks are not responsive to one another's. Each evinces the view from his own private hell. In other words, it's the shame Ernst feels "showering in gym class" that prompts the feeling his "whole life" is "like, some test." That realization is in no way triggered by the thought of Hanschen's hottie, Bobby Maler. Nor does Otto's rejection by Marianna Wheelan prompt Hanschen's sage advice to "kiss some ass." As throughout the show, one character cannot "hear" what another is singing.

"My Junk"
Girls and Boys

In the midst of this nothing, this miss of a life,
Still, there's this one thing—just to see you go by.

It's almost like lovin'—sad as that is.

May not be cool, but it's so where I live.

It's like I'm your lover—or, more like your ghost—
I spend the day wonderin' what you do, where you
 go . . .

I try and just kick it, but then, what can I do?
We've all got our junk, and my junk is you.

See us, winter walkin'—after a storm.
It's chill in the wind—but it's warm in your arms.
We stop, all snow blind—may not be true.
But we've all got our junk, and my junk is you.

Well, you'll have to excuse me, I know it's so off,
I love when you do stuff that's rude, and so wrong.

I go up to my room, turn the stereo on,
Shoot up some you in the "you" of some song.

I lie back, just driftin', and play out these scenes.
I ride on the rush—all the hopes, all the dreams . . .

I may be neglectin' the things I should do.
But we've all got our junk, and my junk is you.

See, we still keep talkin'—after you're gone.
You're still with me then—feels so good in my
   arms.
They say you go blind—maybe it's true.
But we've all got our junk, and my junk is you . . .

It's like, we stop time. What can I do—
We've all got our junk, and my junk is you.

Preparing this song's text for our opening in Seoul in
July 2009, our Korean translator found himself in a

quandary. There was no word, he reported, to convey all the nuance of our "junk." He had to choose, he said, between "joy," "garbage," and "drug." We went with "drug." For, at base, this is a song about addiction.

In the midst of this nothing, this miss of a life . . .

The underpinning of this song is the perception (most elegantly framed by Baudelaire and elaborated on, somewhat insistently, by Proust) that the beloved is herself but "une vase de tristesse," a vase that we fill with the sadness of our own heart. And in filling the beloved, that sad ornament of his nights, with his own longing, the lover fills himself—with the illusion of something to live for.

In Baudelaire's "À une passante," a beautiful stranger passes the poet on the street, and immediately the poet is ready to give his heart, his life, his *all*, to her. For, the beloved (our junk) is really nothing but a vessel that we fill with our own feeling. A phantom we imbue with our passion. A screen onto which we project our longing.

This song originally gave voice only to the yearning of the girls. For them, life is a miss and a thing that's missing—a kind of nonevent. But as we prepped the show for its Off-Broadway premiere, we found that the theme of "junk" also rang true for the boys.

The first set of verses, and the first chorus, give us the girls fantasizing about Melchior and Moritz. The latter verses introduce us to Georg, lusting for his piano teacher, and Hanschen, delirious with desire for a reproduction of Correggio's Io.

For the schoolgirls, the Melchior who passes by is really no more than a ghost. But what they project upon him is so powerful—their drug of choice is so intense— that it seems as if only the beloved is real, and they are themselves his ghost.

This is love as heroin. The terrible addiction to wanting someone. To being unable to stop wanting him. Yes, we try and "kick it"—but, hey, we love our junk.

And, in the idyll, we imagine we are walking in the snow: chill in the wind, but with the drug of love "warm" in our arms.

By allowing our girls a more contemporary lingo, by letting them name this infatuation their "junk," this lyric endows them with a self-consciousness, a lucidity about their situation, which was completely unavailable to the schoolgirls in Wedekind's original play. With the words of this song, our young characters know, even celebrate the fact, that the boys about whom they fantasize are nothing but fantasies. It's as if each girl were saying, "Sure, he may not be the love of my life. But, if life's a nonevent, then I'll take whatever pleasure I can get—and ride the rush for all it's worth."

Naturally, this love is best savored—is only truly explored—when one is alone. Up in one's room, as Hanschen would have it, with the stereo on, hearing in the "you" of some pop song the "you" of the boy one has such an all-consuming crush on. At least the "'you' of some song" gives the jonesing obsessive a momentary fix. Once he gets some of that stuff, he can ride on the rush of all his further "phantasies" . . .

"Touch Me"
Boys and Girls

Where I go, when I go there,
No more memory anymore—
Only drifting on some ship;

The wind that whispers, of the distance, to
    shore . . .

Where I go, when I go there,
No more listening anymore—
Only hymns upon your lips;
A mystic wisdom, rising with them, to shore . . .

Touch me—just like that.
And that—O, yeah—now, that's heaven.
Now, that I like.
God, that's so nice.
Now lower down, where the figs lie . . .

Where I go, when I go there,
No more shadows anymore—
Only you there in the kiss;
And nothing missing, as you're drifting, to
    shore . . .

Where I go, when I go there,
No more weeping anymore—
Only in and out your lips,

The broken wishes, washing with them, to
   shore . . .

Touch me—all silent.
Tell me—please—all is forgiven.
Consume my wine.
Consume my mind.
I'll tell you how, how the winds sigh . . .

Touch me—
—Just try it.
Now, there—that's it—God, that's heaven.
I'll love your light.
I'll love you right . . .
We'll wander down where the sins cry . . .

Touch me—just like that.
Now lower down, where the sins lie . . .
Love me—just for a bit . . .
We'll wander down, where the winds sigh . . .

Where the winds sigh . . .
Where the winds sigh . . .

The shores in these verses derive from my misremembering of Racine's *Phèdre*. Consumed by illicit desire for her son-in-law, the ancient Greek beauty Phèdre calls out to the specter of her ill-fated sister, Ariadne: "My sister, wounded by what love, were you left on lonely shores to die . . ." ("De quel amour blessée / Vous mourûtes aux bords où vous fûtes laissée!") Somehow, in my mind, these shores morphed to a vision Phèdre had of herself, looking down from the imperial height of her censorious mind to the distant shores of her guilty body.

Melchior, Moritz, and all the boys find themselves awash in desire, as they imagine "what the woman must feel"—in the throes of sensual pleasure, "drifting on some ship," hearing only "the wind that whispers, of the distance, to shore . . ." As in my faulty recollection of *Phèdre*, this shore is the shore of the body, of one's own body, of all the material world. It is the shore of the lover's body, glimpsed and remembered from the drifting ship of physical pleasure to which the "I" has surrendered.

"Where I go, when I go there," there is no more "listening": no more conversation with myself—no more the nattering on of daily regret. And, no more "whispering" that one is still *someone*. Rather, there is only the sublime and mystic hymn, the "mystic wisdom" we receive with the kiss . . .

"Touch me—just like that . . ." This stanza, and indeed the imagery of the entire song, is infused with that of the Song of Solomon:

Let him kiss me with the kisses of his mouth—
For thy love is better than wine . . .

The fig tree putteth forth her green figs,
And the vines with the tender grapes
Give a good smell.
Arise, my love, my fair one,
And come away . . .

The figs of our schoolboys' garden, rich to enjoy, are the genitalia of Melchior's essay, transformed (by the pleasure of lovemaking) to a sensual paradise. One by one, the boys fill out the following verses and chorus with longing—and the girls join in, responsively.

Where I go, when I go there,
No more shadows anymore—
Only you there in the kiss;
And nothing missing, as you're drifting, to
    shore . . .

Beyond Munch's remarkable woodprint *The Kiss*, the text that stands behind these verses is Rilke's Second Duino Elegy. There, young lovers lift themselves up to join mouths, "drink against drink" ("Getränk an Getränk"), emerging into one another's caress only to disappear into the kiss.

Where I go, when I go there,
No more weeping anymore—
Only in and out your lips;
The broken wishes, washing with them, to
    shore . . .

"No more weeping anymore," the boys intone, for the life that is not yet here. Our show begins with Wendla hearing "the weeping" among the angels, as she confusedly examines her maturing body. With "Touch

Me," that weeping recedes, overwhelmed by sensuous pleasure. In some enraptured reverie, Georg imagines himself moving in and out that woman's lips—all the broken things he wished for washing away with the tide.

Touch me—all silent.
Tell me—please—all is forgiven.

In other words, Mama may have made Wendla "bad," but "all will be forgiven" in the arms of this love. "Consume every part of me," the boys and girls are saying, "drink the wine of longing, the thought of my mind, and I will whisper in fulfillment, as the winds sigh . . ."

"The Word of Your Body"
Wendla and Melchior

Just too unreal, all this.
Watching the words fall from my lips . . .

Baiting some girl—with hypotheses!

Haven't you heard the word of your body?

Don't feel a thing—You wish.

Grasping at pearls with my fingertips . . .

Holding her hand like some little tease.

Haven't you heard the word of my wanting?

O, I'm gonna be wounded.
O, I'm gonna be your wound.
O, I'm gonna bruise you.
O, you're gonna be my bruise.

Just too unreal, all this.

Watching his world slip through my fist . . .

Playing with her in your fantasies.

Haven't you heard a word—how I want you?

O, I'm gonna be wounded.
O, I'm gonna be your wound.
O, I'm gonna bruise you.
O, you're gonna be my bruise.

Surely, the metaphor of love-as-wound has been with us as long as love itself. I know it first, and best, from ancient Roman poetry: the idea of Venus, or Cupid with his arrows, inflicting some proud youth with an incurable gash. The Latin word is *vulnus*—the root of our *vulnerable.*

But, I have never read elsewhere of a boy or girl sensing that they are soon to bruise one another and become one another's wound. Nor, in most stories, do they wind up, so literally, inflicting wounds on one another (as when Melchior beats Wendla).

As I've written elsewhere, this song functions as the virtual subtext of its scene. Wendla and Melchior discover one another in the woods. And how rare and strange it is, within their world, for a young man and woman to spend time alone together. As they make eager, awkward conversation, they both reflect on the fools they're making of themselves, in the dream of drawing near and "watching the words fall from their lips."

The notion of "the word of your body" probably owes something to Hélène Cixous and her call, in "Le rire de la Méduse," to female authors to liberate themselves from a language that can never express their essence by "writing their bodies": "Écris-toi, il faut que ton corps se fasse entendre."

Melchior and Wendla's bodies confound them with the unintelligible language of desire. And while it all seems too unreal, they know, even on first meeting, all the hurt they will ultimately receive from one another's words and one another's bodies.

"The Dark I Know Well"
Martha, Ilse, and Boys

You say, "Time for bed now, child,"
Mom just smiles that smile—
Just like she never saw me.
Just like she never saw me . . .

So, I leave, wantin' just to hide.

Knowin' deep inside
You are comin' to me.
You are comin' to me . . .

You say all you want is just a kiss good night,
And then you hold me and you whisper, "Child,
    the Lord won't mind.
It's just you and me.
Child, you're a beauty."

"God, it's good—the lovin'—ain't it good tonight?
You ain't seen nothin' yet—gonna treat you right.
It's just you and me.
Child, you're a beauty."

I don't scream. Though I know it's wrong.
I just play along.
I lie there and breathe.
Lie there and breathe . . .

I wanna be strong—
I want the world to find out
That you're dreamin' on me,

Me and my "beauty."
Me and my "beauty" . . .

You say all you want is just a kiss good night,
Then you hold me and you whisper, "Child, the
    Lord won't mind.
It's just you and me.
Child, you're a beauty."

"God, it's good—the lovin'—ain't it good tonight?
You ain't seen nothin' yet—gonna teach you
    right.
It's just you and me.
Child, you're a beauty."

There is a part I can't tell
About the dark I know well.

There is a part I can't tell
About the dark I know well.

There is a part I can't tell
About the dark I know well.

There is a part I can't tell
About the dark I know well . . .

Between our final *Spring Awakening* workshop, in
February 2006, and the beginning of rehearsals Off-
Broadway, we had to dig in our heels a bit and fight to
keep this song in the show. "Wasn't the original source
material dark enough?" I was asked. "Did we really have
to bring incest into the picture?"

The answer was yes—the issue was (and is) too per-
vasive in today's world for us to look away from. And,
as it turns out, this song has resonated with young people everywhere.

Teased by Wendla and Thea, her hair blowing free
on a blustery day, Martha suddenly blurts out to her
friends that her papa beats her. Pressed for details, she
reveals that the man thrusts her out into the cold when
she will not "do as he likes." But only through song do
we learn that, in fact, her papa steals into her bedroom
and makes love to her. This is the part that the young
girl "can't tell."

Martha's is a sad, familiar story: The medicated
mother who smiles in denial, looking right through

her daughter as if she never saw her. The child who somehow blames herself, and cannot bring herself (or himself) to "tell." The child who is undone by her own beauty.

"And Then There Were None"
Moritz and Boys

Uh-huh . . . uh-huh . . . uh-huh . . . well, fine.
Not like it's even worth the time.
But still, you know, you wanted more.
Sorry, it won't change—been there before.

The thing that sucks—okay?—for me,
A thousand bucks, I'm, like, scot-free.
And I mean, please . . . That's all I need.
Get real, okay? By now, you know the score.

You wanna laugh. It's too absurd.
You start to ask. Can't hear a word.
You wanna crash and burn. Right, tell me more.

Okay so, now we do the play.

Act like we so care. No way.
You'll write my folks? Well, okay. Babe, that's how
  it goes.

They're not my home. Not anymore.
Not like they so were before.
Still, I'll split, and they'll, like . . . Well, who knows?
Who knows? Who knows . . . ?

Uh-huh . . . uh-huh . . . uh-huh . . . well, fine.
Not like it's even worth the time.
But still, you know, you wanted more.

Okay, so nothing's changed.

Heard that before.

You wanna laugh. It's too absurd.
You start to ask. Can't hear a word.

You're gonna crash and burn.

Right, tell me more.

You start to cave. You start to cry.
You try to run. Nowhere to hide.

You want to crumble up, and close that door.

Just fuck it—right? Enough. That's it.
You'll still go on. Well, for a bit.
Another day of utter shit—
And then there were none.

And, then there were none . . .

And, then there were none . . .

And, then there were none . . .

Moritz continually feels less than the words he has to express himself; and syntax belongs to a world of stability that he feels has already rejected him. So what is he left with? A kind of desperate staccato of frustrated intention:

Uh-huh . . . uh-huh . . . uh-huh . . . well, fine.
Not like it's even worth the time.

It's not even worth the time to try and express how bad shit gets—how the world has already closed in and turned its indifferent back on him.

But still, you know, you wanted more.
Sorry, it won't change—been there before.

In other words, the anguished Moritz is saying, "My God, why did I bother to go for what I wanted? Like, I didn't know how that would work out?"

Humiliated, disavowed by his father after failing out of school, Moritz has nowhere to turn. At wit's end, he writes to Melchior's mother, the liberal-minded Frau Gabor, asking her for money, so that he can flee to America. She writes back, "I must say straightaway, that fleeing to America is hardly the solution. And even if it were, I cannot provide the money you request."

Moritz traces the elegant evasions of the woman's serpentine locutions. He wants to laugh—to beg to differ. But how can he, really?

You wanna crash and burn. Right, tell me more.

In truth, Moritz blames himself—not only for his failure but for *being* himself. It seems the only way to stop himself is to *stop* being himself. Except, of course, that's too crazy. Or is it?

And then there are his parents:

They're not my home. Not anymore.
Not like they so were before.

Were he not their son, Moritz's parents would never let a boy like Moritz into their home. He's always had to try and hide what he's like, for fear that, if he were exposed, it would come to this.

So, he'll leave. And then what? "Well, who knows? Who knows? Who knows?"

By the song's end, Moritz can hear all his friends in his head, adding their voices to his urgent chant of despair. Then, all at once, it cracks:

Just fuck it—right? Enough. That's it.

What is his life to be but unending days "of utter shit"?

And so, Moritz reaches for his weapon of choice, taking refuge in the old nursery rhyme: "One little Indian boy, left all alone. He went out and hanged himself. And then there were none."

"The Mirror Blue Night"
Melchior and Boys

Flip on a switch, and everything's fine—
No more lips, no more tongue, no more ears, no
*   more eyes.*
The naked blue angel, who peers through the
*   blinds,*
Disappears in the gloom of the mirror blue night.

But there's nowhere to hide from these bones, from
*   my mind.*
It's broken inside—I'm a man and a child.
I'm at home with a ghost, who got left in the cold.
I'm locked out of peace, with no keys to my soul.

And the whispers of fear, the chill up the spine,

Will steal away too, with a flick of the light.
The minute you do, with fingers so blind,
You remove every bit of the blue from your mind.

But there's nowhere to hide from the ghost in my
*   mind,*
It's cold in these bones—of a man and a child.
And there's no one who knows, and there's
*   nowhere to go.*
There's no one to see who can see to my soul . . .

This was one of my earliest lyrics, the second song Duncan and I wrote for the show. The opening stanza sets the scene: A boy (call him, a contemporary Melchior) lies in the dark, haunted by desire. An erotic blue angel peers in the window on him—he feels her lips, her tongue, and her eyes graze his body, and it is all too much—way too hot, and haunting, to handle.

Fraught with regret for the beating he's inflicted on Wendla, Melchior is broken inside—torn between the self who is already a man and the self who is still but a child. He is "at home with a ghost"—for his inner self is haunted by the vision of himself, out there in the cold of the physical world, denied access to peace.

What is there to do but try and silence his fear, to calm the chill up the spine, by turning on the bedroom light? The boy gropes blindly for the switch. As his room is illuminated, the angel disappears into the gloomy blue night. But the light that makes the angel go will leave the boy nowhere to hide—from his body or his mind.

And there's no one who knows, and there's
*   nowhere to go.*
There's no one to see who can see to my soul . . .

"I Believe"
Boys and Girls

I believe,
I believe,
I believe,
Oh I believe.
All will be forgiven—I believe.

I believe,
I believe,
I believe.
Oh I believe.
All will be forgiven—I believe.

I believe,
I believe,
Oh I believe.
There is love in Heaven—I believe.

I believe,
I believe,
Oh I believe.
There is love in Heaven—I believe.

I believe,
I believe,
I believe,
Oh I believe.
All will be forgiven—I believe.

I believe,

(*Left to right*) Thea, Anna, Wendla, Martha, and Ilse: *"Mama, the weeping. Mama, the angels. No sleep in Heaven, or Bethlehem."* (Photo by Tony Snow.)

Professor Sonnenstich: "Moritz Stiefel, *you* are in no position to be taking liberties. I will not warn you again." (Photo by Tony Snow.)

Melchior: "I can hear your heart beat, Wendla." Wendla: "And I hear yours."
(Photo by Tony Snow.)

Moritz: *"So, maybe I should be some kinda laundry line . . ."* (Photo by Tony Snow.)

Herr Knochenbruch: "Melchior Gabor, *did you write this?*" (Photo by Tony Snow.)

Ernst (*left*) and Hanschen: *"O, you're gonna be my wound."* (Photo by Phil Martin.)

I believe,
I believe,
O, I believe,

There is love in Heaven.
All will be forgiven.
There is love in Heaven.
All will be forgiven.

I believe . . .
There is love in Heaven.
I believe . . .
All will be forgiven.
I believe . . .
There is love in Heaven.
I believe . . .
All will be forgiven . . .

Peace and joy be with them,
Harmony and wisdom . . .

Peace and joy be with them,
Harmony and wisdom . . .

I believe . . .

This, too, was one of our earliest songs, originally intended to underscore Moritz's funeral. But we soon cut it, along with all the dialogue there, and the song was all but lost. Then one day, years later, it struck me that we could use the song beneath the lovemaking, underscoring the sex rather than the death.

And, that seemed to work beautifully. "Heaven" found its ironic edge—as the heaven of pleasure (the heaven that Melchior and Wendla will soon find at the feet of Father Kaulbach, at the top of Act Two).

The community of children—almost like hovering angels—assures the young lovers that they will be forgiven what Kaulbach later terms "a grave transgression." But even the innocent can't know for sure. They merely pray that "Peace and joy be with them, / Harmony and wisdom . . ."

"The Guilty Ones"
Wendla, Melchior, Boys, and Girls

Something's started crazy—

Sweet and unknown.
Something you keep
In a box on the street—
Now it's longing for a home . . .

And who can say what dreams are . . . ?

Wake me in time to be lonely and sad.

And who can say what we are . . . ?

This is the season for dreaming . . .

And now our bodies are the guilty ones,
Who touch,
And color the hours;

Night won't breathe
Oh how we
Fall in silence from the sky,
And whisper some silver reply . . .

Pulse is gone and racing—

All fits and starts.
Window by window,
You try and look into
This brave new you that you are.

And who can say what dreams are? . . .

Wake me in time to be out in the cold.

And who can say what we are? . . .

This is the reason for dreaming . . .

And now our bodies are the guilty ones—
Our touch
Will fill every hour.

Huge and dark,
Oh our hearts
Will murmur the blues from on high,
Then whisper some silver reply . . .

And now our bodies are the guilty ones . . .

One winter night in 2007, our first Wendla (Lea Michele) texted me from backstage of our Broadway theater: "Were you thinking about our show when you wrote the lyrics to 'The Guilty Ones'?" She was referring to how our sweet, unknown show had gone longing for a home for years until we finally got it on.

Something's started crazy—
Sweet and unknown.
Something you keep
In a box on the street—
Now it's longing for a home . . .

Lea (as ever) had a point. But I had actually been thinking about something else when I wrote the lyrics; namely, about the guilty longing we all try to keep from ourselves. Wendla and Melchior have found such unfathomable pleasure—love?—in each other's arms.

And who can say what dreams are? . . .

I remember our Austrian lyricist first rendered this as, "Wer weiß schon, was real ist . . . ?" ("Who knows what's real . . . ?") I wrote to her, "It isn't a question for Wendla of what's real but, 'What is this beautiful dream I am going through? Can I trust it? Is it substantive? Will it last?'"

And who can say what we are? . . .

As Prospero states in *The Tempest*, "We are such stuff / As dreams are made on." If we cannot know what dreams are, how can we ever know ourselves?

Sorrow is the shadow of our dreams, for it feeds on the unfulfillment of those dreams. Yet, sorrow also fuels our desire to fulfill them. Like the lover in Shakespeare's rueful sonnet, Melchior asks himself how has he had Wendla "as a dream doth flatter / In sleep a king, but waking no such matter"?

"And now," Wendla and Melchior have heard the word of their bodies, and it is their bodies that are the guilty ones:

Night won't breathe
Oh how we

Fall in silence from the sky,
And whisper some silver reply . . .

The "silver reply" alludes to Shakespeare. When Juliet calls "Romeo" from her balcony, the giddy young Montague replies, "How silver-sweet sound lovers' tongues by night, / Like softest music to attending ears!"

Transported by pleasure from the hayloft where they lie, Melchior and Wendla are like those wonder-wounded lovers in Chagall—falling through the heaven of a wordless love, their bodies whispering, and offering solace, to one another.

Pulse is gone and racing—
All fits and starts.
Window by window,
You try and look into
This brave new you that you are.

Melchior's pulse is racing—such a pitch of excitement that he cannot control himself. It's as if he were running down a street, but the street were the street of himself.

One window after another opens a new vista onto the "brave new" person whom, with each look, he watches himself become.

It's as if, like Miranda in *The Tempest*, Melchior had been kept on a remote island (another form of parentocracy) since his early childhood, and now he were suddenly discovering, as Miranda does, the "brave new world, / That hath such people in't!" But all the people he meets are himself.

"Don't Do Sadness"
Moritz

Awful sweet to be a little butterfly.
Just wingin' over things, and nothin' deep inside.
Nothin' goin', goin' wild in you—you know—
You're slowin' by the riverside or floatin' high and
*   blue.*

Or, maybe, cool to be a little summer wind.
Like, once through everything, and then away
*   again.*
With a taste of dust in your mouth all day,

But no need to know, like, sadness—you just sail
*   away.*

'Cause, you know, I don't do sadness—not even a
*   little bit.*
Just don't need it in my life—don't want any part
*   of it.*
I don't do sadness. Hey, I've done my time.
Lookin' back on it all—man, it blows my mind.

I don't do sudness. So been there.
Don't do sadness. Just don't care.

So maybe I should be some kinda laundry line.
Hang their things on me, and I will swing 'em
*   dry.*

You just wave in the sun, through the afternoon,
*   and then see . . .*
They come to set you free beneath the risin' moon.

'Cause, you know, I don't do sadness—not even a
*   little bit.*

Just don't need it in my life—don't want any part
of it.
I don't do sadness. Hey, I've done my time.
Lookin' back on it all—man, it blows my mind.

I don't do sadness. So been there.
Don't do sadness. Just don't care.

This song was one our director, Michael Mayer, didn't get right away (and this was highly unusual). He didn't understand, for a long while, that it's precisely because Moritz is so consumed by sadness that he denies he "does" it. It is also because Moritz cannot, in fact, *not* do sadness, that the only way to end the sadness is . . .to put an end to himself.

Keats famously asserts in a letter that "A Poet is the most unpoetical of any thing in existence; because he has no Identity—he is continually in for—and filling some other Body—The Sun, The Moon, The Sea . . ."

In other words, the poet scarcely has a self; his own identity is subsumed by the things he sees so feelingly. He disappears, as it were, into the sun, the moon, whatever he observes. In some sense, Moritz yearns to be that poet.

In the waning daylight, with a gun stashed in his pocket, Moritz stands beside the river and gazes out on the world he has never felt a part of. If only he, too, could disappear into that butterfly—could *become* it— then he could be "slowin' by the riverside" without his heart going hopeless and wild within him.

If only he could be some summer wind, blowing "once through everything, and then away again." That is, blowing through the things of life without endlessly having to pause and dwell on everything—without having to second-guess his every move and then fight to suppress the incessant chatter of regret.

Moritz has done time in the prison that is sadness. To go on is only to do more. For Moritz, it's not even worth the effort to care.

"Blue Wind"

Ilse

Spring and summer,
Every other day,
Blue wind gets so sad.
Blowin' through the thick corn,

Through the bales of hay,
Through the open books on the grass . . .

Spring and summer . . .

Sure, when it's autumn,
Wind always wants to
Creep up and haunt you—
Whistling, it's got you;
With its heartache, with its sorrow,
Winter wind sings, and it cries . . .

Spring and summer,
Every other day,
Blue wind gets so pained.

Blowin' through the thick corn,
Through the bales of hay,
Through the sudden drift of the rain . . .

Spring and summer . . .

Spring and summer,

Every other day,
Blue wind gets so lost.
Blowin' through the thick corn,
Through the bales of hay—
Through the wandering clouds of the dust . . .

Spring and summer . . .

This song came so easily. Michael said to me, "Okay, Moritz has a song, now Ilse needs a song, and they should become the same song."

I remember calling Duncan, filling him in on my conversation with Michael and asking, "But do you know how to do that, musically?" "Sure, I don't know, but give me a lyric for her, and I'll figure it out." So . . ."Don't Do Sadness" was in the background of my heart as I wrote the words of "Blue Wind" (words that Duncan set just as I first wrote them, and which we never subsequently revised).

Standing with Moritz, as evening falls over the river, Ilse looks out on the childhood that has already drifted from her—those hours of summer that eternity opens for a moment, when the wind that blows through the lawn before us seems to hold the blue daylight within it.

I suppose Baudelaire's "Chant d'automne" is behind all this. There, the poet hears in the song of autumn all the hard, cold winter ahead. Here, Ilse senses, in the desultory summer, the haunting chant of autumn just around the corner, and the heartache of winter with nowhere to go in the cold, beyond that.

"Left Behind"

Melchior, Boys, and Girls

You fold his hands, and smooth his tie.
You gently lift his chin—
Were you really so blind, and unkind to him?

Can't help the itch to touch, to kiss,
To hold him once again.
Now, to close his eyes, never open them? . . .

A shadow passed. A shadow passed,
Yearning, yearning for the fool it called a home.

All things he never did are left behind;
All the things his mama wished he'd bear in mind;
And all his dad ever hoped he'd know.

O-o-o-o-o-o—

The talks you never had,
The Saturdays you never spent,
All the "grown-up" places you never went;

And all of the crying you wouldn't understand,
You just let him cry—"Make a man out of him."

A shadow passed. A shadow passed,
Yearning, yearning for the fool it called a home.

All things he ever wished
Are left behind;
All the things his mama
Did to make him mind;
And how his dad
Had hoped he'd grow.

All things he ever lived
Are left behind;
All the fears that ever
Flickered through his mind;
All the sadness that
He'd come to own.

O-o-o-o-o-o . . .

O-o-o-o-o-o . . .

A shadow passed. A shadow passed,
Yearning, yearning for the fool it called a home.

And, it whistles through the ghosts
Still left behind . . .
It whistles through the ghosts
Still left behind . . .
It whistles through the ghosts
Still left behind . . .
O-o . . .

The French philosophe Simone Weil wrote that to articulate sorrow is in some sense to relieve it. Something like that sentiment lies behind this song. It struck me that there must be so much in Moritz's father's heart as he stands beside his son's grave, which he will not permit himself even to feel.

With one revision, this song, too, sings precisely as I first gave the lyric to Duncan. (It's a remarkable thing he does, in so often setting my lyrics verbatim: with the exact number of *o*'s and *blaa*s or whatever, that I first give him. I may never understand how he hears within these phrases such precise harmonics.)

The one change I made to this lyric was at Michael's suggestion. The original opening words were, "You scratch your head and wonder why, / He was your little gem." Michael felt that this sentiment was not sad enough. I remember, we had just hung up the phone—I was standing in an airport check-in line, as I quickly wrote the new opening lines: Moritz's father folding his son's hands, and smoothing his tie, as he looks down on the boy in the coffin.

A shadow passed. A shadow passed,
Yearning, yearning, for the fool it called a home.

These lines owe a debt to Homer and the young heroes in his *Iliad* who are struck down in the heat of battle by the "merciless bronze." These slain warriors' spirits depart from them, regretful of the youthful life they are leaving behind.

A shadow passes—the body goes. The shadow—or spirit—passes from Moritz, for whom the body was only a fool within whom he never found a home. And a shadow passes Herr Stiefel, as the poor fool of a child he took for granted departs from his home.

And what is left behind? The regret a father feels for all he never did for his child. These are words I could probably never have written, were I not a father myself.

And, it whistles through the ghosts
Still left behind . . .

The shadow of the ghost whistles through us ghosts. The life Moritz lived, and never lived, are what he's left behind.

"Totally Fucked"
Melchior and Full Company

There's a moment you know . . .you're fucked—
Not an inch more room to self-destruct.
No more moves—oh yeah, the dead-end zone.
Man, you just can't call your soul your own.

But the thing that makes you really jump
Is that the weirdest shit is still to come.
You can ask yourself: hey, what have I done?
You're just a fly—the little guys, they kill for fun.

Man, you're fucked if you just freeze up,
Can't do that thing—that keeping still.

But, you're fucked if you speak your mind,

And you know—uh-huh—you will.

Yeah, you're fucked, all right—and all for spite.
You can kiss your sorry ass good-bye.
Totally fucked. Will they mess you up?

Well, you know they're gonna try.

Blaa blaa blaa blaa blaa blaa blaa . . .

Blaa blaa blaa blaa blaa blaa blaa . . .

Disappear—yeah, well, you wanna try.
Wanna bundle up into some big-ass lie.
Long enough for them to all just quit.
Long enough for you to get out of it.

Yeah you're fucked, all right—and all for spite.
You can kiss your sorry ass good-bye.
Totally fucked. Will they mess you up?
Well, you know they're gonna try.

Yeah, you're fucked, all right—and all for spite.
You can kiss your sorry ass good-bye.
Totally fucked. Will they mess you up?
Well, you know they're gonna try.

Blaa blaa blaa blaa blaa blaa blaa blaa
Blaa blaa blaa blaa blaa,

Blaa blaa blaa blaa blaa blaa blaa blaa
Blaa blaa blaa blaa blaa . . .

Blaa blaa blaa blaa blaa blaa blaa blaa
Blaa blaa blaa blaa blaa,
Blaa blaa blaa blaa blaa blaa blaa blaa
Blaa blaa blaa blaa blaa . . .

Totally fucked!

I always knew these lyrics were mischievous, but I
don't think I realized they would cause such a stir. To
me, the sentiment seemed logical. Melchior stands,
watching his options running out—the grown-ups hold
all the cards, and they're making up the rules as they
go.

In order to protect the reputation of the school, the
headmaster blames Moritz's suicide on Melchior. Unlike Wendla's mother, Melchior answered the questions
put to him about sex, and so he must assuredly be re-
sponsible for his young friend's death.

There's a moment when it sinks in, irrevocably, and
Melchior knows: They're going to get him. No way out.

No time for him even to do like Moritz and "self-destruct." These guys "kill for fun." As Gloucester puts it in *King Lear*, "As flies to wanton boys, are we to the gods."

"The Word of Your Body (Reprise)"
Hanschen, Ernst, Boys, and Girls

Come, cream away the bliss,
Travel the world within my lips,
Fondle the pearl of your distant dreams . . .
Haven't you heard the word of your body?

O, you're gonna be wounded.
O, you're gonna be my wound.
O, you're gonna bruise too.
O, I'm gonna be your bruise . . .

O, I'm gonna be wounded.
O, I'm gonna be your wound.

O, I'm gonna bruise you.
O, you're gonna be my bruise.

O, you're gonna be wounded.
O, you're gonna be your wound.
O, you're gonna bruise too.
O, I'm gonna be your bruise . . .

"The Word of Your Body" articulates such a profound theme of *Spring Awakening* that, for some time, Michael felt its title should further serve as a subtitle for our show. Over the course of the evening, we hear the song three times. First, as Melchior and Wendla sense, in their dangerous attraction to one another, all they may come to mean to one another. Second, as choral underscore, after Melchior has beaten and wounded Wendla. Finally, as Hanschen's siren song to Ernst.

In truth, I first wrote "The Word of Your Body" for the boys. And the lyric was lush with luxuriant promise like that of Baudelaire's "L'invitation au voyage" or the "voluptuous pathos" William Hazlitt found in Edmund Spenser's "Bower of Bliss"—a classic tempter/temptress proffers a sensual paradise to the innocent pilgrim or lovely child. (It was only after our workshop in December 2000 that we realized the potential for Melchior and Wendla's singing "The Word of Your Body" when they first meet. And in June 2001, during our following workshop, we heard Lea Michele and Gavin Creel sing it, and knew immediately we had done the right thing.)

At the tail end of the classroom scene, as the boys head home, Hanschen suggestively proposes to Ernst that they "huddle over the Homer," and "maybe do a little Achilles and Patroclus"—that is, that they privately meet and pore over the adventures of that classic pair of ancient Greek male lovers.

As our show draws to a conclusion, we see those boys together again—this time, by themselves, crouched upon a hillside high above the vineyard, just at sunset. There, in scene and privately in song, Hanschen beckons the awkwardly adoring boy to him, offering the rich dessert of his kiss:

Come, cream away the bliss,
Travel the world within my lips . . .

All Hanschen wants out of life is to "skim off the cream." And if that cream comes with a little boy's heart, then so be it. After all, look how much our golden

young omnivore is offering—all the world within his
lips (to say nothing of the taste of that cream).

Fondle the pearl of your distant dreams . . .
Haven't you heard the word of your body?

O, you're gonna be wounded.

Hanschen first appears to us as Othello. Driven to mur-
derous rage by his chaste girlie postcard, he voices the
words Shakespeare gives his tragic hero, as the raging
Moor enters his beloved's bedroom to do away with her:
"Have you pray'd tonight, Desdemona?" The deed once
done, Othello is consumed by remorse and tormented
by the knowledge that he has thrown away his soul for
all eternity. The once heroic Othello concludes his journey, likening himself to "a base Judean" who has cast
away a "pearl / Richer than all his tribe." Hanschen,
who has crumpled countless paper Desdemonas and
tossed them down his siphon toilet, now taunts one
in the flesh, offering Ernst the chance to "fondle the
pearl of his distant dreams." Like Desdemona, Ernst
will prove true to Hanschen. Like Othello, the rising

young capitalist Hanschen will wound his lover's heart,
but unlike the noble Moor, Hanschen will feel no regret.

"Whispering"
Wendla

Whispering . . .
Hear the ghosts in the moonlight.
Sorrow doing a new dance
Through their bones, through their skin.

Listening—
To the souls in the fool's night,
Fumbling mutely with their rude hands . . .
And there's heartache without end . . .

See the father bent in grief,
The mother dressed in mourning.
Sister crumples,
And the neighbors grumble.
The preacher issues warnings . . .

History . . .

Little Miss didn't do right.
Went and ruined all the true plans—
Such a shame, such a sin.

Mystery . . .
Home alone on a school night.
Harvest moon over the blue land;
Summer longing on the wind . . .

Had a sweetheart on his knees,
So faithful and adoring.
And he touched me,
And I let him love me.
So, let that be my story . . .

Listening . . .
For the hope, for the new life—
Something beautiful, a new chance.
Hear, it's whispering, there, again . . .

This song was with us from near the beginning—I remember lying on the floor of a rehearsal space at La Jolla Playhouse, in the fall of 1999, tweaking and adding verses, to accommodate the music Duncan had written for the lyrics. From that point on, the song was set. No one ever suggested I alter a word of it, until our final, brief rehearsals before our Broadway opening. Through seven years of workshops and an extended run Off-Broadway, Wendla's "Whispering" was a heart-rending lament—an unwed young woman, who's learned she's with child, soulfully regrets that she has become nothing but "another summer's story."

Yes, our song was faithful to the spirit of the original play. But was this the story that, more than a hundred years later, we wanted to tell? Surely, we wanted our Wendla to end her story with something more than tears . . . And so we looked at the song anew, as the conclusion of this young woman's journey; and I reworked the lyrics so that, over the course of the song, Wendla undergoes a transformation.

Whispering . . .
Hear the ghosts in the moonlight.
Sorrow doing a new dance
Through their bones, through their skin.

In her moment of shame, Wendla hears the ghosts—Ibsen's Pillars of Society—in the moonlight, whispering about her. The word of her "shameful act" has prompted a fresh dance of death through their bones.

She stands listening with them, her heart aching for the young fools in love who, like herself, are fumbling rudely, scarcely knowing what they are doing.

Listening—
To the souls in the fool's night,
Fumbling mutely with their rude hands . . .
And there's heartache without end . . .

Wendla cannot yet exorcise herself from the harsh judgment that still echoes within her. Perhaps, like Juliet, she has even a premonition of her own death:

See the father bent in grief,
The mother dressed in mourning.
Sister crumples,
And the neighbors grumble.
The preacher issues warnings . . .

Wendla sees, within her mind's eye, the judgment cast upon her by her family, the clergy, by society.

History . . .
Little Miss didn't do right.
Went and ruined all the true plans—
Such a shame, such a sin.

But as her song continues, Wendla is able to turn from her child language of sin and death to embrace the "mystic wisdom" of what she has felt for Melchior:

Mystery . . .
Home alone on a school night.
Harvest moon over the blue land;
Summer longing on the wind . . .

The song turns, as Wendla does, from the "sin" of what she's done to the "longing" she still feels. Like a child trapped home on a school night, she looks out on the world clothed in shadow and yearns for the summer ahead.

As Wendla's story began, her mother warned her she was "already in bloom." Now she is indeed in bloom, because of the child seeded in her in late autumn, which, sadly, she would have borne in summer.

Had a sweetheart on his knees,
So faithful and adoring,
And he touched me,
And I let him love me.
So, let that be my story . . .

Here, Wendla casts lament aside. She chooses to ignore the ghostly whispers and embraces the growing life within her. More than that, she *owns* those whispers as her story—"Yes, there was a boy, he touched me, and I let him love me. Let that be how I am remembered." Like many a Shakespearean hero or heroine before her, Wendla claims her version of the tale just told, which will be told of her again in times to come.

And so Wendla has journeyed full circle. The young woman who demanded, as the play began, to know how babies are born, completes her journey, listening to the secret whispered to her from the child within her.

"Those You've Known"

Moritz, Melchior, and Wendla

Those you've known,
And lost, still walk behind you . . .

All alone,
They linger till they find you . . .

Without them,
The world grows dark around you—
And nothing is the same until you know that they
have found you.

Those you've pained
May carry that still with them . . .

All the same,
They whisper: "All forgiven."

Still, your heart says:
The shadows bring the starlight,
And everything you've ever been is still there in
  the dark night.

Though you know   *When the northern*
You've left them far   *wind blows,*
  behind—
You walk on by   *The sorrows*
  yourself, and not   *Your heart holds,*
  with them,

Still you know,   *There are those who*
They fill your heart   *still know—*
  and mind,
When they say: *They're still home;*
  "There's a way   *We're still home.*
through this . . ."

Those you've known,
And lost, still walk behind you.
All alone,

Their song still seems to find you.

They call you,
As if you knew their longing—

They whistle through the lonely wind, the long
        blue shadows falling . . .

All alone,
But still I hear their yearning;
Through the dark, the moon, alone there, burning.

The stars, too,
They tell of spring returning—
And summer with another wind that no one yet
        has known . . .

They call me—
Through all things—
Night's falling,
But somehow on I go.

You watch me,

Just watch me—
I'm calling
From longing . . .

Still you know   *When the northern*
There's so much more   *wind blows,*
*   to find—*
Another dream,   *The sorrows,*
*   another love you'll*   *Your heart's known—*
*   hold.*

Still you know   *I believe . . .*
To trust your own true
*   mind.*
On your way—you are
*   not alone.*

There are those who
*   still know—*

Now they'll walk on my arm through the distant
*   night,*
And I won't let them stray from my heart.

Through the wind, through the dark, through the
    winter light,
I will read all their dreams to the stars.

I'll walk now with them.

                  Not gone.

I'll call on their names,

                  Not gone.

I'll see their thoughts
    are known.   *Not gone.*

Not gone—
Not gone—
They walk with my heart—
I'll never let them go.

I'll never let them go.

I'll never let them go . . .

You watch me,
Just watch me,
I'm calling.

I'm calling—
And one day all will know . . .

With this song we completed our transformation of
Wedekind's original story—and with that, of Melchior's
journey. In Wedekind's expressionist original, Moritz
rises from the grave, head in his hands, and beckons
Melchior to join him. Moritz functions, thus, as a per-
sonification of Melchior's despair. In our show, Melchior's lost friends arise within his heart to assure him
they will always be with him, to convince him that life
is still worth living.

Wedekind's Moritz tells his friend that the dead stand
high above—looking down on this world of busy joy
and despair—each alone ("jeder für sich Allein"). Our
Moritz assures Melchior that those we have loved and
lost still walk behind us. Knowing how dark our world
can feel without them, they offer us the consolation of
knowing we have loved them. Those we have loved
and known will never depart from us, so long as we
determine to hold on to them.

Those you've pained

May carry that still with them . . .

All the same,
They whisper: "All forgiven."

Although Wendla still is pained by the memory of all
that has befallen her, she offers Melchior the forgive-
ness promised them (by the choir of children) in the
hayloft. She assures him that "the shadows bring the
starlight"—it is only through the darkness that we dis-
cern the light.

For me, this was always the lesson that the Masked
Man in Wedekind's original play offered Melchior, in
leading him from the graveyard. There may be, within
each of us, a dark we can't tell. But our darkness is not
something to repress or try to flee—how can we escape
what is always there within us? Rather, the darkness is
something to embrace as part of us, something we continually challenge ourselves to transform into the light.

The "northern wind" that our Wendla sings of is
the "inconstant" wind of Shakespeare's *Romeo and
Juliet*, which, Mercutio tells Romeo, "wooes / Even
now the frozen bosom of the north," and "blows us

from ourselves." Throughout medieval literature, the northern wind represents the cold wind of the "Devil King" within our hearts—the part of us that tempts us to despair of being alone.

Here, Wendla assures Melchior that when, as now, he is "blown" from his better self by the memory of sorrow, his friends will still be with him, and offer him a home within them.

Finally, Melchior rises and sings:

All alone,
But still I hear their yearning;
Through the dark, the moon, alone there, burning.

The stars, too,
They tell of spring returning—
And summer with another wind that no one yet
    has known . . .

As our story concludes, Melchior is able to assimilate the voices of his friends—to hear their yearning, and with that to find his place in the world again. He discerns from the position of the stars' constellations the coming of another spring, another summer wind. He determines to live in order to carry his friends' spirits forward—and through the winter light, to read all their dreams to those stars.

"The Song of Purple Summer"
Full Company

Listen to what's in the heart of a child,
A song so big in one so small,
Soon you will hear where beauty lies—
You'll hear and you'll recall . . .

The sadness, the doubt, all the loss, the grief,
Will belong to some play from the past;
As the child leads the way to a dream, a belief,
A time of hope through the land . . .

A summer's day,
A mother sings
A song of purple summer
Through the heart of everything.

And Heaven waits,
So close it seems
To show her child the wonders
Of a world beyond her dreams . . .

The earth will wave with corn,
The days so wide, so warm,
And mares will neigh with
Stallions that they mate, foals they've borne . . .

And all shall know the wonder
Of purple summer . . .

And so, I wait.
The swallow brings
A song of what's to follow—
The glory of the spring.

The fences sway.
The porches swing.
The clouds begin to thunder,
Crickets wander, murmuring—

The earth will wave with corn,
The days so wide, so warm,
And mares will neigh with
Stallions that they mate, foals they've borne . . .

And all shall know the wonder—
I will sing the song
Of purple summer . . .

And all shall know the wonder—
I will sing the song
Of purple summer . . .

All shall know the wonder
Of purple summer . . .

I wrote the first two stanzas of this song at the last possible moment, teaching them to our Ilse, Lauren Pritchard, an hour before our final preview, the night we "froze" the Broadway production. These verses were written to clarify the metaphor of "purple summer" as "a time of hope through the land."

Within the heart of a child, Ilse tells us, there is song: something "so big in one so small." This phrase echoes Christopher Marlowe's "infinite riches in a little room." Marlowe himself is echoing a venerable theological conceit: the Virgin Mary, holding the world's greatest treasure in her fragile human womb. Thus, for me, our prelude to this final song sets out how far we have traveled from the plaintive "Bethlehem" where we began.

As this prelude segues into the song proper, the entire cast steps on to the stage. Setting aside the characters they have played in "some play from the past," they address us as themselves, and tell us of the promise ahead.

And what exactly is a song of purple summer? In general, the initial translations of this lyric (in nearly every language) have been too sentimental and celebratory. For me, "purple summer" represents the time of maturation—a time when the fields will yield crops, and the horses bear foals again. It is the time when the painful spring of adolescence reaches the maturity of summer.

Over the course of the show, we have gone through so much heartache with our characters. We never meant to deny all that with some final anthem. Rather, we wanted to affirm that, in spite of the darkness, life somehow goes on.

I have been asked if the "purple" here refers back to "the wound" Wendla and Melchior have inflicted on each other. To the extent that we carry with us, in maturity, the bruises of our adolescence, it does. But it also represents the purple sunset and the blossoming of the long spring into a summer's day. For all those we have lost, for all that we ourselves have lost, our sorrow will recede, and the earth will burgeon and bear once more.

In a poem I have loved since childhood, Emily Dickinson addresses a "bloom upon the mountain." And though she demurs from naming it, she terms it the "Efflorescence of a Sunset"—for its "solemn petals" reproduce so beautifully the tinge and fragile majesty of sunset.

"Seed had I," she states, "my purple sowing / Should endow the Day." Could the speaker of the poem seed, as does the bloom, she would "endow the day" with her purple. Were the day thus endowed, "Not a tropic of a twilight" would "Show itself away." That is, her purple would be more than the momentary tinge of some departing sun. She, and we, would once more be a part of all that we behold—not merely the observers of that sunset. Like the poem's speaker, we would endow the day with who we are.

Early on, in our classroom scene, Melchior determines to set aside what's "scripted in their Bible" and follow Plato's dictum—to pursue the path of "wonder." As our play concludes, our young characters determine that, through their song, "all shall know the wonder of purple summer."

The swallow is the harbinger of spring. Perdita refers to the spring ahead in *The Winter's Tale*, praising "daffodils, / That come before the swallow dares." As winter passes for our schoolchildren, the swallow sings of what's to follow: Wordsworth's "splendour in the grass, of glory in the flower." A time of sensual fulfillment.

The earth reveals its marvels. A child looks so intently across the lawn, in the heat of a summer's day, that it seems the fences sway and the porches swing.

"And all shall know the wonder": a spring endured, a fulsome time of youth, and a rich purple summer still to come.

April 2011
Los Angeles